The ECE Prep School, LLC

The ECE Prep School, LLC
515 Olive Street, Suite 600
St. Louis, MO 63101

www.theeceprepschool.com

ME!

Ten Poetic Affirmations

By Julius B. Anthony and The ECE Prep School

Illustrated by Kristen Jurgens

ME!
Ten Poetic Affirmations

Inquiries should be addressed to:

The ECE Prep School, LLC
515 Olive Street, Suite 600
St. Louis, MO 63101

www.theeceprepschool.com

First Edition

2 3 4 5 6 7 8 9 10

Library of Congress Cataloging-in-Publication Data is available.
ISBN 10: 1503015025
ISBN 13: 9781503015029

Illustrations by Kristen Jurgens for The ECE Prep School, LLC
Graphic Design and Layout by Rodney Whitley

 # Author's Notes

The ECE Prep School, LLC

This book was written to encourage and inspire. Our desire is for every human being to become aware of the infinite power of courage, hope, and self-love. Let the poems and affirmations in this book nourish you and motivate you to achieve your highest dreams!

We dedicated this book to ten extraordinary teachers from Divol Elementary School, Dunbar Elementary School, and Metro Classical and Academic High School; St. Louis, Missouri:

Ms. Aileen Atwater
Ms. Artemese Bass
Ms. Doris Carter
Ms. Janice Reef-Fleming
Ms. Future Gilleylen
Ms. Heloise Mayer
Ms. Dorothy Richardson
Ms. Camillia Sanders-Banks
Ms. Bettye Wheeler
And the very special Ms. Donna M. Lawton

ME!

No one looks the way I do.
I have noticed that it's true.
No one walks the way I walk.
No one talks the way I talk.

I am special! I am Me!

There is no one!
There is no one!
There is no one!

I'd rather be THAN Me!

I am so glad
to be Me!

Creativity

Hands clap!   Fingers snap!
Head twirl! Feet curl!
Brains think!   Eyes blink!
Knees bend! Arms extend!
Nose smell!   Chest swell!
Voice sing!
Hips – do yo' thing!

We sing... My body's devotion
Creative in motion
Children let your body breathe,
dance, and sing!

Creativity lives in my mind,
in my body, and in my spirit!

Determination

Let all the children affirm.
I am determined to do what is right.
I am determined with all of my might.
I am determined and I feel good about me.
I am determined to be the best that I can be.
I am determined!
Determined!
Determined!
Kujichagulia!

No one can stop me from
achieving, because
I am Determined!

Purpose

(1)
Do you want to know what I can do?
Do you want to know am I true?
Sit on down and
let this phenomenon show you!
I am the hope from yesterday.
I am the truth now.
I am tomorrow's way.
I am PURPOSE!
Yes! That's right!
PURPOSE!
That's me!

(2)
I can call answers from the past.
I can cook and make it last.
I can sing and make the music swing.
When I use my mind, I can do
anything!
I am PURPOSE!
Yes! That's right!
PURPOSE!
That's me!

(3)
I am passionate.
I am peaceful.
I am productive.
I am PURPOSE!
I am soulful.
I am serene.
I am selective.
I am PURPOSE!
Do you want to know who I am?
Do you want to know what I can be?
Open your eyes and
I know you'll see.
I am PURPOSE!
Yes! That's right!
PURPOSE!
That's me!

Heritage

Heritage is,
Our communal past.
Love that last.
Legacy.
Family.
Tradition.
Jubilation.
Celebration.
I have a HERITAGE.

Today I celebrate the legacy of my Heritage!

Unity

Shout!
Unity!
Together in verse!
Shout!
Unity! Me and the universe!

When I obey my parents, and strive to do good.
I'm working together with the universe just as I should.
When I go to school, listen and learn everyday.
I'm working together with the universe
in a very special way.
When I aspire,
and I dream to be all that I can be.
I'm working together with the universe
to set free the beauty that is living inside of me.

So I shout!
Unity! Together in verse! I shout!
Unity! Me and the universe!

I live in harmony and unity with all living
and non-living things
around Me!

Abound

We need abundant love.
To lift us.
Free us
Keep us.
Revive us.
I have abundant love.

We need abundant peace.
To calm us.
Clear us.
Balance us.
Contain us.
I have abundant peace.

We need abundant joy.
To enliven us.
Expand us.
Propel us.
Fulfill us.
I have abundant joy.

We need abundant faith.
To defend us.
Strengthen us.
See us.
Release us.
I have abundant faith.

Everything I need I already have
in abundance!

Decidedness

Someone said I couldn't do it.
It would be too hard for me.
I said, "Ok, you will see. I will climb the tallest tree."

Someone said I couldn't do it.
You are too small.
I said, "Ok, I will show you all. I can scale the thickest wall"

Someone said I couldn't do it.
You are too weak.
I said, "Ok, just watch me sail the widest sea."

Someone said I couldn't do it.
You aren't that strong.
I said, "Ok, how many times are you going to sing the same old song?"

Never tell me what I can't do!
I am the one who will see IT through!

Courage

I am - Courage.
I am the substantiation of self-belief.
I am the evidence that excellence exist.
I am the personification of
purpose and possibility.
I am the representation of resilience.
I am the image of Imani.
I am the proof of patience and persistence.
I am - Courage.

I can beat all the odds
because
I have courage!

Believe

I believe when you are kind to others,
Others will be kind to you.
I believe when you believe,
All of your dreams can come true.

I believe in me and all of my abilities.
I believe when you believe,
You can create your own opportunities.

I believe in love as the master plan.
I believe when you believe,
Love can make you say "I can"!

I believe in the need to look beyond what I can see.
I believe when you believe,
It is your courage that will set you free!

I believe. Yes! I believe.

No one can shake what
I believe!